2019

Emory,

We are hoping this book will keep the Lakes memories fresh, until you can be here again.

We love you,
Pere + John
Grizz

Whispers on Winnipesaukee

A Haley Mae Story

This Book Belongs To

_____

"If she's old enough to go to school,
she's old enough to come to New Hampshire
for a summer with us," said Aunt Fizzie.
"I couldn't agree more," said Mimi.
And so she did.

WATCH FOR FUTURE
HALEY MAE STORIES...

www.SisterSpiritBooks.com

Whispers on Winnipesaukee

A Haley Mae Story

AUTHOR
"MIMI"
MARTHA KRUSE

ILLUSTRATOR
"AUNT FIZZIE"
PHYLLIS L. STIBLER

Whispers on Winnipesaukee: A Haley Mae Story
Copyright © 2017 by Martha Kruse and Phyllis Stibler
ISBN 978-1-934582-69-5

All rights reserved. No part of this book may be reproduced or utilized in any form or by any means, electronic or mechanical, including photocopying, scanning, recording or by any information storage and retrieval system now known or hereafter invented, without permission in writing from the publisher. Inquiries should be addressed to:

BACK CHANNEL PRESS
220 State Road, #336
Kittery, Maine 03904
www.backchannelpress.com

Printed in the United States of America

Book design by Nancy Grossman

Library of Congress Number 2017955453

"What's a copyright, Mimi?" asked Haley Mae.

"A copyright is a form of protection for original works of authorship and artistic expression," explained Mimi, "so nobody can steal your writing or your artwork."

"Gee, I write and draw a lot. Should I get a copyright?" Haley asked thoughtfully.

Giants, Witches, and other Unlakely Creatures

"I want to explore some of the islands on Lake Winnipesaukee," said Haley Mae, once her bags were unpacked at Mimi's house. Haley's name for her grandmother has always been Mimi. "How many islands are there, anyway?" she asked, licking the maple syrup from her upper lip. Blueberry pancakes are her favorite breakfast – at least this summer.

"Well, that's a bit of a trick question. The answer depends on who's defining what an island is," Mimi responded. "Would you believe . . . more than two hundred?"

"Wow, we better get going then!" Haley exclaimed.

"We won't be able to see them all – at least not in one visit," Mimi laughed, "but before we cast off for the islands, have you wondered about the name of the lake, Winnipesaukee?"

"It's a funny name, Mimi. I can't even spell it. What does it mean?"

Whispers on Winnipesaukee

"Ah, I've piqued your curiosity, have I?" Mimi smiled. Haley squinted and giggled. "Look! The girl with the piqued curiosity peeks at me!" Mimi laughed.

"Long before the European settlers came to New Hampshire," Mimi told Haley, "the native peoples, a group of many tribes known as the Abenaki Nation, gave names to the lakes, rivers, and mountains. The original name means 'lake where there are other lakes and ponds.' The Abenaki name helped people find their way — let's say the way to the weirs — before there were maps. Winnipesaukee is the biggest lake in the whole state — and this is a state with 959 of them!"

Haley's eyes widened with surprise. "Wow!" she gasped. "But Mimi, I learned about American Indians in school, and I thought they lived in Colorado — like me. Do the islands have Indian names, too?"

"Well, there *is* Gichigumi. And some others sure have unusual names. Try these on for size: Overnight Island. Spider Island. Rattlesnake, Upper Shoe, Little Barndoor, Sleepers. Bear, you know. The smallest island is called Becky's Garden. It's only ten feet wide — a little bit smaller than your bedroom. Its size changes depending on the level of the water in the lake." Mimi paused, giving Haley time to think about where water comes from.

"My dad told me that rainfall and snowmelt from the Rocky Mountains make the lake near my house full in the springtime," Haley chimed in proudly.

Giants, Witches, and other Unlakely Creatures

"Those events play a part in the water level in Lake Winnipesaukee, too," smiled Mimi. "There is another factor, also, called lake management. Come on, let's walk down to the boat dock."

"Seriously, Mimi? How can you manage a lake? Lakes are part of nature."

Haley got a far-away look. She imagined great blue giants, their arms and legs wrapped in strings of green seaweed, linking their bulging arms together to form a ring around the edges of a lake. She could hear the giants grunting and groaning as they struggled to keep the water level just below their armpits. When the water splashed into their noses their groans sounded like a train whistle.

WHISPERS ON WINNIPESAUKEE

Haley's eyes abruptly flew open when she realized it *was* a train making those ear-piercing sounds. The Hobo Railroad train chugged toward them, making its return trip to the Weirs.

"Who does – what's the word? – manage the lake?" Haley yelled to Mimi over the clickety-clack made by the massive train wheels. Kids waved happily from Leo's Party Caboose as it chugged past the entrance to the dock.

"It's complicated," Mimi answered. "A group of people have studied and learned about all of the lakes in this region. They developed a plan that protects the natural beauty of the water and shoreline. The plan also protects wildlife habitat, and allows people to boat and swim and even land airplanes on the lake. Lake management requires lots of people working together. I am thankful that people care about New Hampshire's lakes and take steps to protect them."

Mimi could see Haley working to assemble the pieces of that puzzle in her mind. She took Haley's hand and said, "Let's go find where Grandpa's docked and do some exploring of the lake."

Haley jumped aboard the flat deck of Grandpa John's pontoon boat. Mimi pushed the vessel away from the dock. "Where to, First Mate Haley?" Grandpa asked.

Giants, Witches, and other Unlakely Creatures

"You know, silly Grandpa! Sally's Gut, of course," laughed Haley, "and then on to Bear Island!"

"Ahoy, then, mates! Hold on tight!" Grandpa pushed the throttle forward. The boat moved at wake speed away from the dock, then sped off as it reached open water.

Haley snuggled down into the cushy seat in the bow of the boat, smiling as the wind whipped through her hair. "Why are there black and white sticks in the water?" she asked, turning to Captain Grandpa.

Whispers on Winnipesaukee

"Those are called markers. They show us where there are big rocks we can't see," Grandpa explained. "Those markers protect us from accidents and from running aground. The lake management team drains water out of the lake in the fall to allow room for the snow. In the fall we see all kinds of boulders that we didn't know were there."

"What if you're out on the boat and it gets dark?" Haley asked with a worried look. "You can't see the sticks – I mean markers – in the dark."

Grandpa pulled out a big map. "This is a chart of the lake," he explained. "It shows you where all the islands and the rock outcroppings are. Would you believe one of the big rock groups is called the Witches?" Grandpa made his scary noise.

Haley wasn't fond of witches. They had a habit of appearing on people's lawns right around the time of her late October birthday. Visions of ugly old hags with warts on their noses appeared in her mind. She cringed at their harsh cackling. Conjuring up all of her powers of imagination, she magically changed the horrible witches into beautiful mermaids whose gentle whispers lulled her into sweet dreams.

"What happened, Mimi?" she asked, finding herself leaning against Mimi's shoulder, not quite sure how she got in that position.

Giants, Witches, and other Unlakely Creatures

"We've entered the channel that goes through the Weirs and opens into the big lake," Mimi said. "The rules of the road – excuse me, of the lake – are that you slow down when you see the orange and white markers that say 'No Wake.' Those markers are called buoys."

"Oh, I remember this bridge!" squealed Haley. "Can I beep the horn, Grandpa?" Not waiting for his answer, Haley slid off her seat and rushed back to the helm in time to hear the "meep meep" of the horn echoing off the bridge walls.

EYES OUT FOR ISLANDS

"Watch out for the ducks, Grandpa! You won't hit them, will you?" Haley yelled anxiously. "By the way, what's a weirs?" Haley never ran out of questions.

"That's a great question, Haley," Grandpa replied. "Not about the ducks. Don't worry, they're very good at getting out of the way of boats. About the weirs. The Abenaki set up villages along lakes and rivers and used traps called weirs to catch fish. Thousands of people came to this very spot for the yearly spawning of shad, salmon, and alewife."

"Alewife! That's a silly name," said Haley. "Look, there's an island straight ahead!" Haley shouted with glee.

Eyes out for Islands

Water splashed Haley in the face as the boat lurched forward into the big lake. Blinking the water out of her eyes, she noticed the puffy clouds overhead. They looked like animals racing across the bright blue sky.

Just as she was about to ask where clouds come from Grandpa slowed the boat again. Turning her gaze from the sky to the waterline she saw what she had been dreaming about since visiting New Hampshire two years before: Sally's Gut!

WHISPERS ON WINNIPESAUKEE

"Slow down, Grandpa," pleaded Haley and Mimi. They leaned over the edge of the boat to look for treasures on the shallow bottom of the narrow stream. Haley loved the way the clear water curved around the land.

Eyes out for Islands

"Look, there are houses on this side of the Gut, but not on the other side. Why don't people live there? Can I see Sally's Gut on the map – I mean chart? Oh, look! There's a turtle on a log!"

Questions and observations tumbled out of Haley's mouth faster than a loon can swim under water.

"The side with no houses is Stonedam Island."

"I remember hiking on Stonedam Island!" exclaimed Haley. "When an owl whispered to me. Or was that just a story you made up for me, Mimi?" Mimi just smiled.

"Stonedam Island is owned by the Lakes Region Conservation Trust," Grandpa continued. "No houses can ever be built on it."

"You mean people own islands?" interrupted Haley.

"Yes, they do," Grandpa went on, "which is why the person who owned this property sold it to the Trust. That person wanted this beautiful island to be protected. He knew the Conservation Trust would be good stewards of the island."

Before she could even ask, Grandpa explained, "To be a steward means to plan and manage resources in a responsible way. In this case we are talking about taking care of the natural world."

"Are there stewards in Colorado?" asked Haley hopefully. "I want somebody to protect where I live, too."

"There are acres and acres and thousands of acres of protected land where you live, Haley. Hopefully, all states will listen to kids like you and protect natural areas for the benefit of wildlife and people," concluded Mimi.

The pontoon boat floated past the last "No Wake" buoy, and took off toward open water. The shimmering blue of the lake and the deep green of the trees that covered the shore looked nothing like Colorado. Haley began to feel a little bit sad. Was she homesick? Climbing onto the driver's seat with Grandpa, she began to feel a little bit better.

"Would you like to help me steer the boat?" Grandpa asked.

"Can I? Am I old enough?" asked Haley, feeling a little concerned.

"You have to be sixteen to get a boat license, but you can help me drive to Center Harbor," assured Grandpa.

Eyes out for Islands

"What's Center Harbor, and why are we going there? I thought we were going to Bear Island." Now Haley felt a little confused.

"You'll see," said Grandpa, and forced the boat to its highest speed.

SURPRISE PASSENGER

"Aunt Fizzie?" screamed Haley, jumping up and down as the boat approached the Center Harbor town dock. "That's Aunt Fizzie standing on the dock! Yay! You said I'd see her this trip."

"The one and only," said Mimi, jumping in unison with Haley.

"Hey, you two, you're rocking the boat," teased Grandpa. "We call Aunt Fizzie our very own bird whisperer – which means she can just about talk to birds of all kinds. In fact, she just finished a morning of training at the Loon Center in Moultonborough. She'll be full of fascinating information about loons."

"I remember the loons from my last visit to New Hampshire," Haley said joyously. "Remember how they stood up on the water and flapped their wings. And when they dove, the way they came up in different places. I pretend I'm a loon sometimes when I'm swimming at the pool.

A Surprise Passenger

I don't tell any of the other kids that though. I don't want them to think I'm loony!" Haley giggled at her own joke.

Aunt Fizzie's big straw hat almost blew off into the water as she leaped aboard the pontoon boat. Haley took a flying leap off the seat into her auntie's arms when she was safely aboard.

"You are almost too big to catch anymore, my little Colorado Kitten," said Aunt Fizzie, shifting her weight to regain her balance as the boat took off. The crew of four headed for Bear Island.

"I've been missing you, Aunt Fizzie," sighed Haley as she gave her auntie another giant hug. "Can we go find some loons?"

"You can never be certain where you will find the loons on this huge lake," said Aunt Fizzie, "but I have learned a lot about them while training to be a field volunteer."

"You go to a field to see loons?" asked Haley. "I thought they can't fly very well and have to stay in the water."

"A field volunteer goes wherever they are needed. In the case of loons, the 'field' is the lakes. I help monitor the number of loons, report injured or dead loons, and check for unhatched eggs. I also build and float nesting rafts, watch over nesting loons, and teach people how to enjoy the lake while not endangering the loons."

"You see dead loons, Aunt Fizzie? That's so sad." Haley looked like she was about to cry.

"It is sad. But the good news is that the loon population is slowly recovering. By recovering, I mean that the number of loons is growing because some very alert people noticed that the number of loons in New Hampshire was becoming smaller, and people needed to act quickly.

"Part of the problem is the activities of people using the lakes. We can all live together and enjoy the lakes, loons and people, if we are careful and thoughtful," smiled Aunt Fizzie. "Oh, I almost forgot, I brought you something from the Loon Center store." She went digging in her backpack, pulled out a small bag and handed it over to Haley.

Haley ripped into the bag, pulling out a pair of black and white socks, with a red stripe. "These are crazy socks, Aunt Fizzie," Haley offered, a little unsure of what else to say.

"When we spot a loon, you'll understand," smiled Aunt Fizzie confidently.

"Well, you're in luck," said Grandpa John. "Loon pair off the starboard bow."

Grandpa took the motor out of gear. The boat drifted quiet as a whisper toward the loons. As the loons came into

A Surprise Passenger

view, Grandpa and Aunt Fizzie adjusted their binoculars. "We have to be careful not to drift closer than a hundred fifty feet," said Grandpa in a hushed voice.

"Yup, there's a chick on the back of one of the loons," observed Aunt Fizzie. "We need to be careful not to cause stress for the parents."

"We'll back away even further if they signal," assured Grandpa John. "They let you know when you're too close. And if they swim away from us, we *never* follow them."

"Oh, look. The baby dove under the water," exclaimed Haley. "I can't believe a little baby loon chick can do that. I was five years old before I could hold my breath under water. Didn't you say that babies hatch in early July?"

"The chicks can dive when they are just a few days old, but they're like little corks – they pop right back up to the surface," Aunt Fizzie explained with a chuckle. "It's kind of funny, thinking of little loon chicks popping up out of the water, but by the time they're three months old they can dive, catch fish, and feed themselves. Sometimes that's when their parents migrate – they fly away. Somehow the babies figure out what to do," Aunt Fizzie continued.

A silence fell over the boat as each of them thought about the differences between bird families and people families.

At last, Haley said, "I love loons, but I am glad I am a person and not a loon."

"I agree," said all three adults at the same time.

"What's that commotion on the water?" asked Mimi, sounding alarmed. Something was clearly in distress.

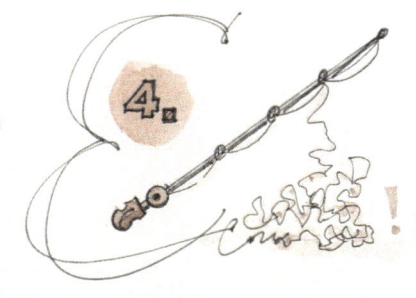

LOON IN DISTRESS

Grandpa guided the boat cautiously toward the spot Mimi pointed to. Haley was first to identify the problem. "It's a loon, turning over and over. Something's wrong with it," Haley cried out in dismay. "I think it's going to drown,"

"I see the problem," sighed Aunt Fizzie. "The loon is tangled in fishing line."

"We have to rescue it!" cried Haley. "We can reach down, scoop it up, and lift it into the boat," Haley exclaimed, "and then we can cut the fishing line."

"We don't have the equipment to do that," said Aunt Fizzie, shaking her head.

It soon became clear that Haley's plan might not work. Each time the boat came close to the struggling bird, the loon dove under the water, well out of reach. The already stressed bird was made even more anxious by the would-be rescue team.

"Oh, no," wailed Haley. "The loon is going to die. There aren't enough loons as it is."

"There's only one thing we can do to save this bird," said Aunt Fizzie. She reached for her phone and called the Loon Preservation Committee. "If we're lucky, the biologist is still there and will come out in a boat to help this loon."

Aunt Fizzie's voice echoed across the water as she explained to the biologist the location of the frantic bird. Hanging up the phone she said, "He's on his way."

"Can we wait?" pleaded Haley. "Maybe we can help."

"We can help by staying out of the way," explained Mimi, "but we can stay close by."

After what seemed like a very long time, a small boat approached the pontoon boat. Haley pointed to the nearly exhausted loon, now barely moving in the water. She held her breath as the biologist made his first reach for the bird with a large net.

"Oh, no, he missed," Haley sighed. The boat made another pass. Haley watched as the man tried again to capture the hopelessly entangled bird.

Loon in Distress

"What happened?" asked Haley with a puzzled look. "He almost had it in his net."

"Loons have strong pointed beaks," explained Aunt Fizzie. "This bird doesn't understand that the biologist is trying to help it. It's trying to defend itself with its best weapon, its beak."

Haley felt hot tears streaming down her cheeks. She whispered soothing words to the enormous bird. "It's okay, Mister Loon, let the man help you," she said quietly.

Everyone on the boat was holding their breath, hoping the biologist could help the loon and not be injured by the loon's sharp beak. Finally, he was able to scoop the bird in his large net and bring it aboard the boat.

"I'm afraid the man is going to break the loon's wing," Haley wailed, hurling herself into Mimi's lap.

"No, look, Haley," Mimi said. "He was able to cut one section of fish line with the cutters! Oh, yay! Now he's cut another."

The biologist gave everyone the thumbs up. "This bird seems healthy. I think you found it shortly after it got tangled in the line. Just the same, I'm going to take it to shore so a vet can examine it before we release it. Thanks so much for your help."

Haley waved goodbye to the biologist as he steered his boat toward Center Harbor. "Thank you, Mister Biologist!" she yelled gratefully. "Goodbye, Mister Loon!"

"I'd call this a high-five moment, wouldn't you, Haley?" said Aunt Fizzie. Four sets of palms met in the air with a solid smack.

Cozy Coves and Cucumbers

"Here we are in Deep Cove, one of many coves on the shoreline of Bear Island," said Grandpa John. "First Mate Haley Mae, will you help Mimi with the lines as we tie up at the docks. These docks belong to St. John's-on-the-Lake Chapel. It's one of our favorite spots to dock, eat lunch, and take a little hike."

"Bear Island is one of the largest islands of all," explained Mimi, "but it's not connected to the mainland by any bridge. There's only one way to get to it."

"Yep, boat or swim!" said Grandpa. "And the shortest distance is almost a half mile. That's a long swim."

"Can we swim before we eat and hike?" asked Haley, already taking off her swimsuit

27

cover-up. "I remember how we climb down the ladder in the back of the boat to get in the . . . Yikes, this water is cold!"

"Cold and refreshing," said Aunt Fizzie, already making her way down the ladder, too.

Mimi and Grandpa John followed reluctantly. They had lots of experience convincing themselves that swimming in cold water is fun. As usual, they were the last ones in and the first ones out. Finally, Haley climbed up the ladder, teeth chattering.

"Thank you for the socks, Aunt Fizzie. It's cold sitting here in a wet bathing suit. Oh, I get it, the socks are the same colors as the loons! Black and white, with red like their red eyes. I never saw a bird with red eyes before. What's in that picnic basket, Mimi?" Mimi started pulling out lunch.

"Can I throw my bread crusts in the water for the ducks?" asked Haley, after gobbling down her sandwich.

Cozy Coves and Cucumbers

"Actually, that is not a good idea," said Aunt Fizzie. "I'll give you three reasons why bread is not good for ducks. When ducks eat human food that isn't healthy for them, the ducklings don't learn how to forage healthy food for themselves."

Haley looked puzzled. "Forage?"

"Find food on their own," said Mimi.

"Oh, okay. Forage," Haley smiled. "And the other two reasons?"

"Second, when ducks eat the wrong kind of food they can produce babies with a wing deformity call 'angel wing.' Those babies can't fly very well. The third reason is that uneaten bread crumbs can contribute to the growth of algae blooms in the water that are bad for the lake."

"Is there any people food that is good for ducks?" asked Haley.

"Believe it or not, vegetables like cucumbers, peas, broccoli, tomatoes, pineapple, and flowers are safe for ducks and other water birds," answered Aunt Fizzie.

"Some of your favorite foods," smiled Mimi.

"Except for the flowers," laughed Haley. "Do cucumbers make ducks burp like they make Grandpa John burp?" she giggled, squirming away from Grandpa so he couldn't tickle her.

"B-u-u-r-r-r-p," Grandpa pretended loudly. "Let's go hiking. Put on your hiking shoes. The trail is a little rocky. It is New Hampshire, after all."

"Wow," said Haley, a little breathless after the climb. "What's that crazy building doing here in the middle of an island?"

"That's the Bear Island Chapel," explained Grandpa. "It's ninety years old."

Cozy Coves and Cucumbers

"That's old," said Haley. "It looks like a church."

"It *is* a church. It's only open in the summer. Remember, people can only get here by boat, or on foot if they live on the island," Mimi explained.

"What else is there on the island besides a church and houses?" Haley asked.

"Let's go back to the boat and we'll show you," offered Grandpa John.

"It's a long way around this island, Grandpa," remarked Haley as the boat chugged on.

"That's true, Haley. See that dock there on our starboard side?"

"To the right, right?"

"That's right. See the little building on the dock? That's the post office."

"A post office like where you take your mail? It the tiniest post office I've ever seen," said Haley skeptically. "The post office where I live is huge! Wait, if you can only get to Bear Island by boat, how does the mail get here?"

"I am so glad you asked that question," laughed Grandpa. "A boat named the *Sophie C* has delivered the mail to Bear Island for fifty years. In fact, she delivers mail to eight islands on the lake during the summer.

WHISPERS ON WINNIPESAUKEE

The kids on one of the islands, Birch Island, perform skits – you know, like plays – for the mail boat as it passes by. One of the kids always ends up in the water during the skits, I'm told. I bet the passengers on the *Sophie C* get a kick out of watching someone fall in the lake."

"That sounds like fun," smiled Haley. She wondered what it would be like to live on an island. Were there bears on the islands? What about Bear Island?

"Bear Island has no bears on it," Grandpa said. Haley perked up. Did she ask him a question, or was he reading her mind? Grandpas are like that.

"It is nearly three miles long and three-quarters of a mile wide," Grandpa John went on. "Here we are."

"What's this? It looks like fun," said Haley.

"This is a camp. Girls spend the night here. There's another camp on the island just for boys. There are lots of overnight camps on Lake Winnipesaukee," said Mimi.

"How do all of these camps fit on one lake?" asked Haley, looking a little bit mystified.

"The lake covers seventy-two square miles, and with all the islands there is lots of room for houses and camps of all sorts. Maybe you would like to attend a camp on the lake some day," Mimi suggested.

Cozy Coves and Cucumbers

"Would I ever!" Haley shouted as she hopped up and down, sending a seagull squawking across the water. Overhead, a bald eagle's white head gleamed in the afternoon sunshine as it rode the warm air currents rising up over Red Hill.

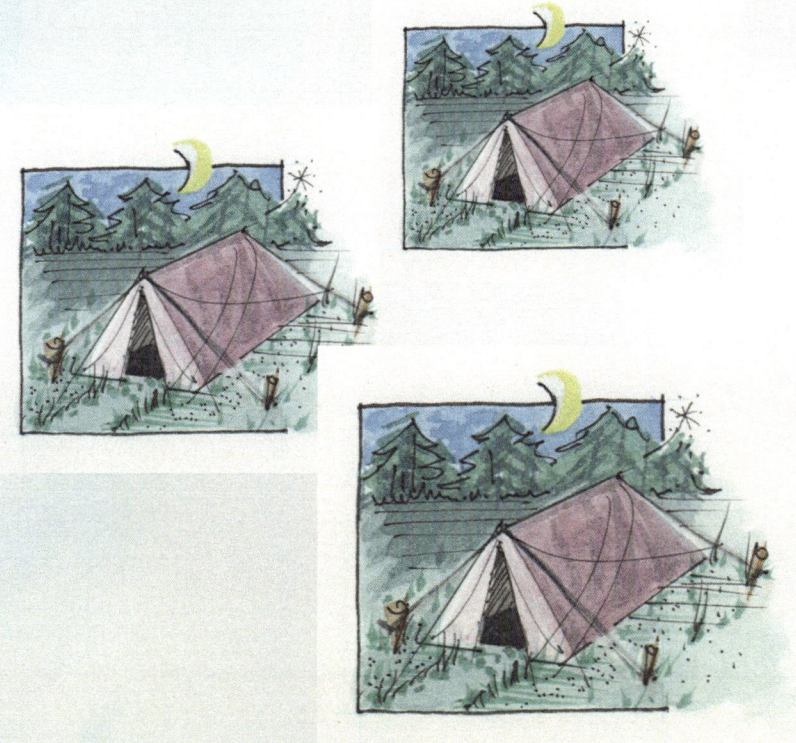

"Where to now, Grandpa John?" asked Haley.

"It's been a long day, Haley," said Grandpa. "I think we'll head home. Perhaps we'll see something else of interest on the way. You never know what might cross your path on Lake Winnipesaukee."

Haley was pondering that possibility when Aunt Fizzie suddenly pointed excitedly at a ship heading towards them.

"It's the *Mount Washington*," said Mimi.

"It's ginormous!" said Haley. "Where did it come from?"

"It appears to be on its way from Wolfeboro," said Mimi.

"Maybe we can race it back to the Weirs," exclaimed Aunt Fizzie.

"I don't think so," said Haley laughing. "It looks like it is going pretty fast. And it's so big!"

Cozy Coves and Cucumbers

"It's two hundred thirty feet long," said Grandpa, "and it totally overpowers us. We'll just see how we do."

"Even if we lose the race, we still have a bonfire and s'mores to look forward to after dark," Haley stated with confidence. "Right, Grampa John?"

"Right you are, First Mate Haley," he assured her.

"And there's another surprise, Haley. Aunt Fizzie offered to give you a lesson in painting with watercolors," Mimi chimed in.

"That'll be the perfect end to a perfect day on Lake Winnipesaukee," Haley squealed. "Thank you all so much!"

"Thank you for being our so adventurous granddaughter!" laughed Mimi and Grandpa John.

"And my whimsical niece!" smiled Aunt Fizzie.

Haley eagerly crawled into bed after her day on Lake Winnipesaukee. She tried to remember all the things she had learned about the lake, its islands, and its wildlife. She was eager to impress her family with her new-found knowledge and the paintings she had created with Aunt Fizzie's help.

Try as she might, Haley couldn't stay awake. She dreamed that Aunt Fizzie whispered to her that she could come stay with her on the New Hampshire seacoast when she visited next summer. Actually, Aunt Fizzie really did talk to her about swimming in the ocean and visiting lighthouses, and holding starfish and sea cucumbers at a science center.

Cozy Coves and Cucumbers

"Tomorrow I am going to ask Aunt Fizzie if there really are cucumbers in the ocean," Haley promised herself as the gentle whisper of a Winnipesaukee breeze coaxed her to sleep.

THE  END

GLOSSARY

bow - the front of the boat (pronounced like cow)

conservation - protection of the natural environment

deformity - a body part with the wrong shape

habitat - the natural home of an animal, plant, or other living creature

helm - a steering wheel on a boat

pique - spark curiosity

pontoon boat - a flat-bottomed boat with floats

port - the left side of the boat

spawning - releasing eggs

starboard - the right side of the boat

wake speed - the boat moves without creating waves behind it

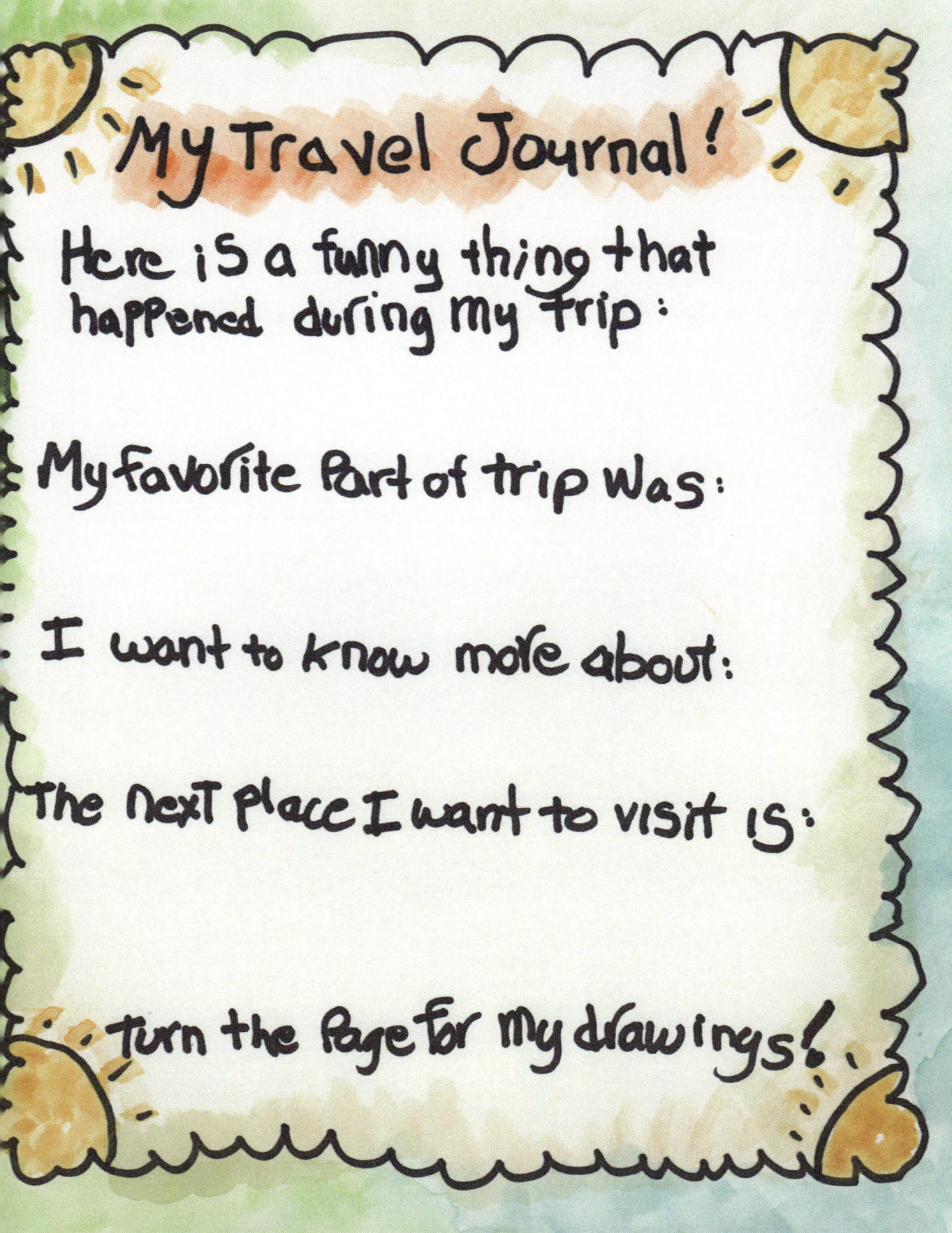

my drawings!

ACKNOWLEDGMENTS

AUTHOR

Appreciation to Paul W. Pouliot, Sag8mo & THPO, Cowasuck Band of the Pennacook-Abenaki People, for taking the time to clarify and authenticate the original meaning of the name, Winnipesaukee.

Appreciation to the staff at The Loon Center in Moultonborough, NH, for their assistance in the description of a loon rescue.

Kennedy, you gave the journal page a special caché, and your insightful questions led to greater clarity in the text. You read well beyond your ten years.

John, your support, suggestions, and enthusiasm have been amazing.

Appreciation to our editor and publisher, Nancy Grossman, for your encouragement from the beginning. "Thanks, Ed!"

ILLUSTRATOR

Appreciation to Brian Reilly, President of the Board of Trustees, Loon Preservation Committee, for his inspiring photographs.

Appreciation to Jennifer Lee for her illustration guidance.

Appreciation to Jeff, Adam and Chloe Byrd for making my life full of fun and adventure.

ABOUT THE AUTHOR

Martha earned her MEd at the University of Maryland. A retired special educator from Hopkinton, NH, she worked as Specialist in the Assessment of Intellectual Functioning (SAIF.) The Haley Mae stories came to life at the request of her granddaughter. Martha lives in Laconia, NH, with her husband, where she enjoys tennis, pickleball, and – of course – Lake Winnipesaukee.

ABOUT THE ILLUSTRATOR

Phyllis holds a BFA in Interior Design from Syracuse University School of Art and has enjoyed a 45-year career as a commercial interior designer and founder of Stibler Associates Space Planning and Interior Design LLC. She now combines her rendering skills and a love of watercolors with another long enjoyed interest – children's books. She lives on Great Island, New Castle, NH.

Martha and Phyllis have been dear friends since meeting in college in 1970. They enjoy traveling together and the creative process of making stories come alive for children of all ages.